C000043322

A wondrous, nonlinear, pote
has counted every syllable, co
where it hurts the most." Each poem bursts and expands beyond
its scale, moving you through a measured wormhole of body and
life. "I am the garden/ Eve never took back," Samuels writes, "Fist
with-/in the bone, rising." Grounded in a practice and form that
began for the poet out of everyday necessity, Samuels applies
pressure on language to create "solid beings," offering them to us
now as *Hypermobilities*. I love this book.

Oliver Baez Bendorf
author of *Advantages of Being Evergreen*

Ellen Samuels's *Hypermobilities* is a crip gift to the universe. Not
only documenting precisely and acutely the daily moments of a
sick life, Samuels bends and creates new genres out of disabled
times and spaces, on purpose--succinct words emerging from the
MRI tube, the bed, the diagnostic non-process. Samuels writes a
body's language I have wanted and needed to read, a crip force of
sparse stars and disabled imagination rooted deep in the body and
land's soil. Thank you so much for writing it.

Leah Lakshmi Piepzna-Samarasinha
author of *Care Work: Dreaming Disability Justice*

The patience and acuity of *Hypermobilities* spin the haiku—its
little aerated ideogram (Barthes)—into koan, vignette, playground
taunt, and fragment hymn. Its disarming, deceptively minor
gestures hold a torch to pain's bruising quotidian. I am glad to keep
company with Samuels's bracing endurance art of attention.

Michael Snediker
author of *The Apartment of Tragic Appliances*

hypermobilities

poems

ellen samuels

the operating system's unlimited editions
in corpore sano **print//document**

hypermobilities

ISBN: 978-1-946031-93-8
Library of Congress Catalogue-in-Publication Number: 2021944278
copyright © 2021 by Ellen Samuels
interior and cover design by Elæ Moss

is released under a Creative Commons CC-BY-NC-ND (Attribution, Non Commercial, No Derivatives) License: its reproduction is encouraged for those who otherwise could not afford its purchase in the case of academic, personal, and other creative usage from which no profit will accrue. Complete rules and restrictions are available at: http://creativecommons.org/licenses/by-nc-nd/3.0/

For additional questions regarding reproduction, quotation, or to request a pdf for review contact operator@theoperatingsystem.org

Typography: This text was set in Millemetre, OCR A Std, Minion and Europa. Millemetre, our title font, is used via a SIL Open Font License, through Velvetyne Type Foundry. It was designed by Jérémy Landes. All type on VTF is libre and open-source, and fully aligned with the OS's mission. Support their work and learn more at https://velvetyne.fr

Image description: the cover shows the book title, HYPERMOBILITIES: POEMS and the name ELLEN SAMUELS against a background of abstract art in red, gray and steel blue with black line drawings creating layered patterns of honeycomb cells, kelp-like neurons, and map grids. The art is drawn from "Molecular Route" by Laura Jacobson. See more at http://laurajacobson.com

As of 2020 all titles are available for donation-only download via our Open Access Library www.theoperatingsystem.org/os-open-access-community-publications-library/

The Operating System is a member of the **Radical Open Access Collective**, community of scholar-led, not-for-profit presses, journals and other open access projects. Now consisting of 40 members, we promote a progressive vision for open publishing in the humanities and social sciences. *Learn more at:* http://radicaloa.disruptivemedia.org.uk/about/

Your donation makes our publications, platform and programs possible! We <3 You http://theoperatingsystem.org/subscribe-join/

the operating system
www.theoperatingsystem.org
IG: @the_operating_system
tweettweet: @the_os_

hypermobilities

acknowledgements

I'd like to thank early readers and listeners to these poems who helped me believe they could become a book: the hosts, producer, and audience of Wisconsin Public Radio's Central Time; the generous organizers and co-readers in the Watershed series at the Arts and Literature Laboratory in Madison, WI; Jesse Lee Kercheval, Judy Mitchell, and all my colleagues in the Creative Writing Program and the Department of Gender and Women's Studies at the University of Wisconsin-Madison; Oliver Baez Bendorf, Michael Snediker, Leah Lakshmi Piepzna-Samarasinha, Alison Kafer, Timothy Yu, and all my beloved NADs.

I also owe many thanks to the talented poets who have been my teachers over the years: Bruce Beasley and Wendy Hesford at Oberlin; Ken McClane and the late A. R. Ammons at Cornell; and most of all, Barbara Helfgott Hyett, who taught me more than anyone about how to write, revise, and publish poems.

I am deeply grateful to Elæ Moss and The Operating System for giving this work a place in the world and to my OS cohort for sharing their brilliance with me.

All my love to my sweet son Charlie and to Jonathan Zarov who fills my life with love, humor, and songs, and brings me cold things when I can't get out of bed.

I would also like to extend my profound gratitude to the many doctors, nurses, medical assistants, front desk staff, orthotists, physical therapists, lab workers, and radiology technicians who did not know they were being written into poems as they inserted IVs, administered injections, operated MRI machines, brought me blankets, listened to my fears, and comforted my pains over the past seven years and counting. I hope you recognize some piece of yourselves in these poems also.

To my crip community: you saved my life and continue to save me every day. From you I have learned that disability and illness, though often terribly lonely, can also be the way we find community, the way we find family, the way back to our own truths. I thank you for my survival and I dedicate myself to yours.

contents

I. hypermobility

II. symptoms and signs

III. coloring the pain book

IV. narcissus

V. prognosis

VI. the garden

***

I. hypermobility

Hypermobility

No one is supposed
to bend that far. No one knows
why you don't just break.

Beighton Hypermobility Scale

Thumb, wrist, palm on floor.
All the ways you go too far.
Tally up your score.

The Difference Between
Joint Subluxation and Dislocation

Door unlatched in the
body-house. Shudder to slow-
kiss the jamb. Or slam.

Hypermobility of the Small Joints

To press a button
means fingers muscle past bone.
Yes, No, Enter, Yes.

Hypermobility of the Large Joints

If your legs were wings
they'd need to swing this far out.
And feathers. And sky.

Don't climb a hill, then
pick up leaves. Too much bending.
I mean, ambition.

Hypermobility of the Large Joints 3

The ankle joint is
connected to the leg joint…
That's enough for now.

II. symptoms and signs

Nausea

Not stomach but throat.
Gravel-stuck throat. Throat a fist.
Throat gnawed clean to bone.

Fatigue and Malaise, Nonspecific

Eight hours of sleep,
not enough for you. Maybe
you dream too slowly.

Nausea with Vertigo

Feet slip on rocking
deck. Slosh of belly. Climb the
mast of your throat, dive.

Palpitations

Heart-door, stop swinging.
The storm has passed. Only you
still ravage and spark.

Delayed Gastric Emptying

Too-full elevator
returns to top. Toast, butter,
juice. Unhungry heart.

Vertigo

The world we're on
is always spinning. Maybe
you're just standing still.

Vertical Up-ticking Nystagmus

Let yourself be seen.
Cornea naked as skin.
Up. Up. Try to fly.

III. coloring the pain book

⫴ 32 ⫴ ⟊

At the Doctor's Offices

Tell me who I am.
What day I was born. Don't ask.
Tell me why I'm here.

Tylenol with Codeine

If pain like a taste
could be rinsed and wrung, swallowed
all tongue-clean and new.

Magnetic Resonance Imaging
of the Head and Neck with Contrast

When the dye begins
to flow through the needle, don't
move. Don't think aloud.

Magnetic Resonance Angiogram
of the Head and Neck with Contrast

There are blue rivers
running your skull-lines. Hold so
still you can feel them.

Subluxation, Shoulder

The smallest pop. Un-
stopped, what you knew and forgot
in this knife-joint caught.

Bath with Epsom Salts

If the giant who
held the sky could for once lie
down in this warm sea.

Yellow burning. Red
stabbing. Black numb. Draw a star
where it hurts the most.

IV. narcissus

Narcissus on His Illness

Is a poem like
a mirror, or pond, or both
ways to drown and see?

Vertebral Artery Dissection

If while you slept the
walls peeled open, the red light
burst in everywhere.

Infusion: Ondansetron 4 mg.

Quick dip of needle,
blood-taste before grace. Slow push
to hold you for days.

Unmentionable

Shitting is daily
exercise. Muscle, breath, clench,
let everything go.

Infusion: Normal Saline 500 ml.

Ocean, seagrass, spill
of sand into tourniquet,
needle, mermaid hand.

Infusion: Magnesium Sulfate 1 g.

Element body.
Planet's core. And you, the vein
that opens and pours.

Superficial Phlebitis

Needle-mouth, vein-road, the
price that was paid. What healed, hurt.
What hurt is what stayed.

V. prognosis

Genetic Testing for the COL3A1 Mutation

We would know this by
your face, heart-shaped, lucent. So
why ask the shy blood?

Genetic Testing for the COL5AI Mutation

One letter typed wrong.
One plate chipped. Blood-deep in you,
one petal drifting.

Autosomal Dominant Inheritance

This body knows what
your mother did not—what
she gave, this body.

Atrophic Scarring

Cut-off breast, cut-out
belly, did no one notice
her night-blooming skin?

Cigarette-Paper Scarring

So she rolled into
surgery, split apart, came
out still spreading still

Unidentified Mutation of BRCA-1

In a photo of
your mother, you a gray blur,
a smoke-wisp, a sign.

No one knows yet how
to carve skin from scars, to live
knife-backwards to now.

VI. the garden

Displacement of the First Rib

I am the garden
Eve never took back. Fist within the bone, rising.

Early Blight

What dirt remembers
the leaves know also. Leopard
yellow, growl of spots.

Swan Neck Deformity of the Fingers

How far must you bend
this time, all the way backward
to birth, that lost grace?

Pruning Tomato

Snip at the stem-joint.
Feel where it hollows. Only
the bent wrists will fruit.

Harvesting Carrots

It all comes down to
who wants more, the roots to stay
or you to break them.

Ankle Sprain, While Sleeping

Warm swell of pain, foot-
knuckle bruising. What dance did
you dream and forget?

Thinning Carrots

Tug-root, tendril, let
go. Slide free as words from lips.
This is not your earth.

Notes on Writing Hypermobilities

When I began composing these poems in my head, I was lying stiffly in the rigid embrace of an MRI machine. I didn't think at the time I was writing poems for anyone else to see; I was only thinking, *how do I get through the next minute, the next hour, week, day, year of this?* I was only beginning to learn how to keep living when I might die any second, my left vertebral artery a wayward twig split down to its green.

***

For a head and neck MRI, you lie flat on your back with a white-ribbed mask strapped over your face to hold your head perfectly still. The underside of the mask is sticky like old car upholstery. You close your eyes against it, eyelashes brushing its smooth skin. Then you feel the tech's hand like a friend passing a secret note, tucking the rubber bulb of the emergency cord into your palm.

"Squeeze this if you need us, OK?" she murmurs, and you try to nod but the mask stops your head from moving even a millimeter. So you say "Thanks!" as loudly as you can, your hearing muffled from the earplugs she pressed in your ears before buckling the cage. Then you feel your body slide into the tube, like a suitcase disappearing on an airport conveyor belt, like a quart of milk down the check-out aisle, like a tray of fresh rolls into an oven.

Everything is white in the machine, the ceiling and sides and lights, but all you see with your eyes closed is deep plum-brown, bright flickers of egg-yolk yellow, after-glows of the overhead glare you left behind. Under the press of mask you can feel the separate shape of each eyeball, felted marble against the lid's thin scrim. Then the tech's voice startles the darkness: "We're beginning now. Don't move."

The noise of the machine is always louder than you remember: CHA WHOOP CHA WHOOP BANG BANG BING BANG

BANG. Jackhammers destroying the sidewalk outside your Oakland apartment window. The iron radiator's midnight clangs in your hundred-year-old college dorm. BANG BANG BING BANG. Your nose is starting to itch. "Don't move."

You start to say words in your head.

> *Sound poem of the MRI.*
> *Sound poem of the/ MRI.*

"We're starting the contrast. If you stop the test now, we'll have to start again from the beginning. Don't move."

> *When the dye begins to flow through the needle, don't move.*
> *Don't think aloud.*

You say the words over and over, forcing them into neat lines. You make them fit, counting the syllables behind your eyes.

> When/ the/ dye/ be/gins
> to/ flow/ through/ the/ needle/ don't
> move/ Don't/ think/ a/loud.

Five syllables, seven syllables, five syllables. The way you were taught to write haiku in Cumberland Elementary School in 1978, a poetic form adopted (stolen?) from another culture and turned into a kind of poetry that you don't usually hear taken seriously anymore. A kind of poetry you yourself have not taken seriously.

But that's why you can do it now, in the machine, without pen or paper, without screen or keyboard. Without thinking anyone else will ever hear the words outside the dark closed room of your own mind.

***

My diagnosis with an spontaneous vertebral artery dissection at the age of forty-two was a singularly dramatic moment in a lifetime of mysterious illness. In childhood I had a series of strange maladies and bodily differences: my legs always hurt, I caught every bug, I couldn't sleep at night or stay awake during the day. Things other people could do, ordinary things, were as impossible for me as flying: snapping my fingers, whistling, blowing a strawberry-flavored gum bubble. My body bent where it was supposed to stay firm and froze solid in the places it should bend. My mother paraded me from doctor to doctor but the most they would say was *more exercise*. It wasn't until my early twenties, soon after my mother's death from cancer, that these bodily oddities worsened to the point where I struggled sometimes to walk or eat or button a shirt. So I began my own lonely search for answers.

Like many chronically ill people who have the privilege of access to medical care, I saw dozens of doctors and acquired many theoretical and half-true diagnoses before I was finally diagnosed with the genetic condition Ehlers-Danlos Syndrome, a connective tissue disorder caused by a defect in the synthesis of collagen, a protein woven through all the critical systems of the body. EDS finally offered a unifying answer, a map to all the crumbling arteries and overpasses in my bodily metropolis.

I was diagnosed first with Hypermobile EDS, now called hEDS, the most common type of EDS. But when I was referred to a geneticist to confirm the diagnosis, he brushed his fingers over my bruised and "doughy" skin and declared that I looked more like a mild form of a rarer type, Classical, a.k.a. cEDS. He ordered genetic bloodwork for known mutations of cEDS and, even though it came back negative, he wrote it down as my diagnosis anyway. The genetic tests were not conclusive and it was his best guess. And, since all we could do was treat my symptoms, he said it didn't really matter what type I had.

That is, as long as we knew I didn't have Vascular EDS, the only type that kills without notice. A vEDS body is so fragile that vital organs can spontaneously rupture or *dissect*—the first time I heard that term to describe a process that sounded terrifying but not relevant to me. This reassuring narrative lasted about six years, until I had my first head and neck Magnetic Resonance Angiograph in 2014, searching for the cause of my increasingly debilitating bouts of vertigo. A few days after the scan, I received a brief note from my doctor that the results were normal, as so many of my tests were, despite all my body's evident failures.

Then, almost three weeks later, my phone rang on a Friday night. Even though it was my doctor's number, I didn't pick up, assuming it was merely her office robot reminding me of an appointment. But then I saw she had left a voicemail, telling me to check MyChart.

In MyChart I found this message:

> Dear Ellen,
>
> Neuroradiology re-read your scans and found that you have a 3 mm dissection in your left vertebral artery. A dissection means a small tear in the inner wall of an artery. You should start taking 325 mg of aspirin right away and I have sent a referral for you to be seen in neurology. In the meantime, if you have any symptoms such as weakness on one side of your body, difficulty moving or speaking, or paralysis, please go to the emergency room right away.
>
> Yours, Dr. R.

I read and re-read each sentence, trying to understand what was happening. I thought we had ruled out any chance that I was at risk for dissections, that my diagnosis simply wasn't serious enough for that. As I took a long breath in, I was vividly aware of my heart knocking against my breastbone, its echo on the side of my neck.

Searching the internet, I learned that an artery dissection is an emergency, as the briefest interrupted flow of oxygenated blood to the brain could cause permanent, even life-ending damage. Usually a person with an artery dissection would be rushed to the ER and hospitalized. But since radiology had missed the dissection on my MRA for almost three weeks, it surely made no sense to treat this as an emergency.

But, then, what was it exactly? I texted my partner, who was out playing lead guitar in a rock and roll show, and asked him to pick up a bottle of aspirin on his way home.

I soon learned that living in a state of *not-not-an-emergency* meant a deluge of mixed messages, medical appointments, and MRAs. Since most vertebral artery dissections completely heal within three to six months, my new neurologist kept ordering scans to check on its progress. Each time he told me it showed no signs of healing, I burst into uncontrolled and embarrassing sobs. Eventually he stroked his balding head and, without looking directly at me, allowed as how some dissections just never heal.

That first year I also underwent genetic testing to rule out vEDS and a range of other deadly disorders and spent countless more hours in MRI machines having my entire body scanned for hidden aneurysms. The angiogram of my chest was particularly difficult. I was called back to the hospital the next morning to get clearer scans of my heart which had a troublesome habit of beating when it needed to stay still. As the technician's voice boomed in my ear, *don't move, don't breathe*, I pressed my lips together till my jaw's hinge ached, willing my pulse to stop so they could see my heart and let me go. In the end, the new tests found nothing else, only that one stubborn strip of paper peeling off my artery's wall.

Meanwhile I was told to go to the emergency room whenever I felt dizzy—but I was dizzy almost every day. After the bright and tedious terror of my third ER visit in a month, I decided to cope with my dizziness at home instead. I stopped calling my neurologist's office with questions because they would always *always* tell me to go to the ER. Get another MRA. Get the same answer—"Your dissection is stable and unchanged"—without any actual treatment for the vertigo which worsened under the stress until some days I could barely sit up.

Eventually I found a headache neurologist who now treats my vertigo as migraine-related— maybe related to the dissection, maybe not? Because of the dissection, though, it's too risky for me to use any of the most effective medical treatments for migraines. Even regular intravenous infusions of "safe" medicines help just a little and not for long (and trust me, I've tried every alternative treatment under the sun, from butterbur capsules to energy manipulation).

So over the past six years, worsening vertigo and related neurological symptoms have drastically changed my already non-normative chronically ill life: I went from working as a college professor full-time to part-time to total medical leave from my beloved job; from crisscrossing the country to visit family, give talks, and go to professional conferences to rarely leaving my house; and from living mostly independently to becoming increasingly dependent on my partner and paid helpers when I am too dizzy to get out of bed for days at a time.

It was during this time that I began, haltingly, after many years' hiatus, to write poetry again. The haiku I would compose in my mind during MRIs, infusions, nerve blocks, and other medical procedures helped me pretend I had some control over my life and body as they slipped further into chaos and loss. I didn't think at first about publishing these poems. I didn't expect for a long time that anyone would want to read or publish them. Now that the book is being published, I feel both grateful and a little afraid, like I've been turned inside out for everyone to see.

***

Two years after my dissection, I faced another terrifying specter of my body's betrayal. My brilliant and beloved mother had died at age fifty-two of ovarian cancer after surviving breast cancer two decades earlier. The year after her death, researchers identified mutations on the BRCA gene that raise the risk of breast and ovarian cancer so staggeringly high that it has become standard treatment for carriers of the mutation to have risk-reducing surgeries to remove their breasts and ovaries. Although doctors immediately began pressing me to be tested for the BRCA mutations, I resisted for many years, waiting until more was known about their risks, as well as for legal protections to be passed so that a positive test would not ruin me. When I finally agreed to be tested, my results—like my genetic testing for cEDS—were inconclusive, or as the genetic counselor put it, "uninformed negative." In other words, while they did not find a known BRCA mutation in my DNA, it was still quite likely, based on her history, that my mother had an unknown mutation and I could have inherited it. On the other hand she might have had a known mutation that I had managed to evade. Since she died before testing was available, there was no way to know for sure. My doctors told me that risk-reducing surgeries could still be advisable and put the decision in my hands.

My research into mastectomies for people with EDS then led me to a startling and heart-piercing discovery: my mother's broad, jagged mastectomy and hysterectomy scars, which I had assumed were typical, were in fact the characteristic atrophic or "cigarette-paper" scars of cEDS: too wide, too thin, new skin like papier-mâché stretched over gaps it could never quite fill.

My own lack of atrophic scarring had always been the reason my diagnosis of cEDS never quite made sense. Did this mean that, if I had surgery, those scars would appear, another secret gift from my mother hidden deep in my cells? Nearly unable to bear what were now twin burdens of genetic risk and uncertainty, I was sustained by the unwavering love of my partner, my family of beloved friends, and the queer and disability communities from whom I had learned that my body would be sacred despite—and even because of—my scars, seen and unseen.

Finally, as the age of my mother's fatal diagnosis loomed, I chose to undergo surgical removal of my ovaries and fallopian tubes to address the far more deadly risk of ovarian cancer while relying on a routine of intense surveillance for breast cancer. My surgery was done laparoscopically through my navel so I still don't know if my skin will ever bloom those paper-white scars, if those questions will ever be fully answered.

***

Sometimes when I lie in my dark bedroom with its closed curtains I think about what I want to tell people about being chronically ill: that it's both worse and better than you think it is. That I don't want to be pitied but I also don't want to pretend everything is okay. Like any person, I simply want to be seen in the actual reality of my experience. I suppose that is what I hope these poems can do: show my particular ill experience to the world while side-stepping the unbearable reactions of *I'm so sorry. How do you do it? This makes me so sad for you. You are so strong!* And at the same time to offer my words to other sick and disabled people, to say: you are not alone. And neither am I.

So many of the stories we tell and are told about illness try to flatten it, to draw as simple a line as possible from onset to diagnosis to recovery, cure, or death. The everyday details are left out as we rush to the dramatic reveals. I am guilty of this impulse as well; I'd never claim to be immune to the seduction of plot. But I also know that for many of us there is no plotline, no arc toward either cure or tragic end— merely the endless strum of illness's wax and wane.

So while this book arcs from a beginning to an end, an arrival of sorts, it resists any kind of recovery or overcoming narrative. The story I want to tell is a different one. I want to show that people with chronic illness are not simply hollowed-out vessels whom sickness fills like water. We are solid beings, living sick lives, every day, every minute, and those are lives also, with every grain of complexity and richness and truth as lives that are not sick. And I wrote these poems not only out of my sickness but out of my entire life, voicing my experience all the way down to its depths, even though those depths are shaped at every mark, in every sediment, by what it means to be sick.

So again and again, as I turned inward to my body, to the white-walled rooms of the hospital where I spoke these poems into existence in my mind, I found the words themselves turning me outward again. I started writing about my injured first rib and found that I was writing about Eve in her garden. So I went out into my garden and then found myself writing about my wrists and finger joints. I fed myself on the words I wrote and I wrote the sustenance I needed to keep living, every day, even the days when I could not lift my head from the pillow without feeling myself atop the mast of a great ship, ready to plunge into the depths below.

And eventually I began to let go of the idea that the poems I was writing were not real or good enough to share with the world. I began to read them in public sometimes, to share them on social media, to ask people I trusted to tell me if they could become a book. I am deeply grateful to those early readers and listeners, and to Elæ Moss and the Operating System, for letting me know that these poems have work to do in the world, a work that does not have to be about prestige or form or about proving anything except this: that I lived, *I survived*, and I wrote these poems.

And now I am giving them to the world, to you. Thank you for reading them, and for being here in this world with me.

ELLEN SAMUELS is a professor of Gender & Women's Studies and English at the University of Wisconsin at Madison and author of *Fantasies of Identification: Disability, Gender, Race* (NYU Press, 2014). Her writing on disability can be found in academic forums like *Disability Studies Quarterly, Signs,* and *GLQ,* and in literary journals like *Copper Nickel, Brevity, Rogue Agen*t, and *Mid-American Review.* She has received the Catherine Stimpson Prize for Outstanding Feminist Scholarship and two Lambda Literary Awards. She lives in Madison, WI with her partner, son, and dog.

about the artist: Laura Jacobson

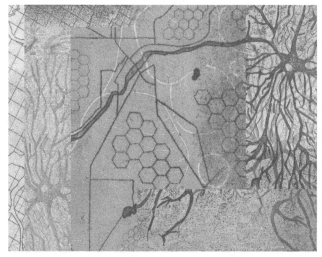

Our cover uses a special digital variation made for this project by the artist of her original work, "Molecular Route." (Monoprint, chine-collé, BFK paper, 2018)

Laura Jacobson began using neuroscience in her printed and sculptural artwork in 2011 when she was given MRIs of her brain after volunteering as a research subject in a scientific experiment. In "Molecular Route", from her series *Topography of Being*, the artist draws on imagery from neuroscience and road maps to make etchings on paper that are cut and collaged. The work depicts astrocytes, the most abundant cells in the central nervous system, which play a vital role in the connections and sustenance of the brain's billions of neurons. The honeycombs refer to grid cells, considered the brain's GPS, firing electrical pulses in a hexagonal lattice while humans move through space. Aligning a 1920s Automobile Blue Book route map with astrocytes and grid cells, the work grapples with systems in the brain responsible for memory, perception, and navigation. Jacobson holds a BA from Stanford University and an MFA from the Rhode Island School of Design. Her ceramics and prints may be found in private collections, including NYU Langone and Stanford University. She maintains a sculpture and print studio in Palo Alto, CA.

https://laurajacobson.com

welcome, I want to know you
an OS [re:con]versation with Ellen Samuels

Greetings comrade! Thank you for talking to us about your process today! Can you introduce yourself, in a way that you would choose?

I am a queer disabled poet, a white cis woman, a professor, a parent, a disability studies scholar, and a person living with Ehlers-Danlos Syndrome.

Why are you a "poet"/ "writer"/ "artist"?

For as long as I can remember, writing has been the thread along which my life was strung, the way I most naturally and deeply expressed myself and connected with the world. But there came a time when I was twenty years old, when my beloved and brilliant mother was dying quite horrifically from cancer and I was one of her main caregivers for those last months with no hospice or nursing support. At that point, for me, writing became about survival. It was and still is the one thing that I cannot live without and that shows me how to keep living even when faced with the unlivable.

When did you decide to use the language you use for yourself?

I wrote poetry since I was a child, but I don't think I ever called myself a poet until I started my M.F.A. And then it wasn't something I chose for myself exactly: you were either in the poetry or fiction program and I was in the poetry program so I was a "poet." But then, after I graduated and published a small chapbook of poetry, I stopped writing poetry for a long time while I did my Ph.D. and became a disability studies scholar, got a job in that field, and wrote an academic monograph. I am very comfortable calling myself a scholar. To call myself a poet still feels a bit strange. But I suppose I am that now.

What's a "poet" (or "writer" or "artist") anyway?

Ideally, it's a person who uses their art, their words, to draw meaningful and surprising connections between their inner selves and the world around them. And there are many different ways people do this. I admire spoken word poetry so much, and I think it does this tremendous work in the world that the poetry we see coming out of M.F.A programs and being published in literary journals doesn't necessarily do. But much of that poetry is also doing really important work.

I do think that unless you don't try to publish at all, or you only self-publish, you have to contend at some point with Poetry Inc., the poetry-industrial complex, and figure out what your relation will be to it-and if you have to have some kind of relation to it in order to call yourself a poet. I am thinking a lot right now about what my relationship to Poetry Inc. will be, and whether I can participate enough to connect with other people whose work is so transformative and valuable, but without getting caught up on the hamster wheel of prestige and competitiveness.

What do you see as your cultural and social role (in the literary / artistic / creative community and beyond)?

I write about disability. I've always written about disability, pretty much as soon as I myself really became disabled, which was actually during my M.F.A. program when I was in my early twenties. And I am very committed to and embedded in disability community, by which I mean a political community, a cultural community, not one primarily defined around a certain diagnosis or impairment. So that will always be who I write for, first and foremost.

I have worked quite hard, but I have also had a tremendous amount of privilege—racial, economic, educational privilege—that helped me succeed in my career as a disability scholar so that now I am a full professor at a major university. And that's still true even though at this point I am quite ill and can rarely even leave my house or even get out of bed some days. So although I still feel like a relative novice in the current world of creative writing publishing after my long hiatus, I also acknowledge that a lot of doors are opened to me by the privilege and the position I have. While of course I want to get my work out there and promote it, I am also committed to using my privileged access to uplift other disabled writers, especially BIPOC writers, trans and nonbinary writers, and writers who are untenured or contingent or independent from the academy. Most disabled people in this country live in forced poverty and I don't, so it feels very important to me to redirect resources to other disabled writers as often as I can. I see that as one of the most important things for me to do at this stage in my career.

Talk about the process or instinct to move these poems (or your work in general) as independent entities into a body of work. How and why did this happen? Have you had this intention for a while? What encouraged and/or confounded this (or a book, in general) coming together? Was it a struggle? Did you envision this collection as a collection or understand your process as writing or making specifically around a theme while the poems themselves were being written / the work was being made? How or how not?

At the beginning, as I talk about in the essay about writing this book, I didn't think these were poems for publication at all. They were quite literally a survival practice, something I started doing in my head to sustain and distract me during MRIs, IVs, ER visits, and all the wretched bodily symptoms that were taking over my life: dizziness, pain, nausea, etc. I would compose them in my head and then later post them on social media to friends only, or scribble them on bits of paper. I don't remember the point when I started putting them all into a word document. But at some point I did, and I started to accumulate quite a few of them, and one day I realized, I'm writing a book. And it really only works as a book, as a complete narrative, which is why I call it a verse memoir. I sent out some of the poems to journals and I had no success at all, none, getting them published. Some of the journals would say, send us something else, and I would send a more recognizable poem, a longer free verse poem, and that would get published. But the haiku, I realized, only worked as a complete book and eventually over many revisions, I ended up with six sections that each have seven poems. I had a lot more poems than that, maybe about two dozen more, but they didn't all fit into the book for one reason or another.

What formal structures or other constrictive practices (if any) do you use in the creation of your work? Have certain teachers or instructive environments, or readings/writings/work of other creative people informed the way you work/write?

I have had some wonderful poetry teachers and companions over the years. To be honest, most of them were not at my M.F.A. program, which was at Cornell University, so it was a very rarified space and in the early 1990s, a space that was just starting to include queer writers or writers of color in any meaningful way. Many of my fellow students were just wonderful writers and I learned a lot from them, but the program itself was a fairly hostile place for me. The same was actually true for the creative writing program at Oberlin College where I was an undergraduate before Cornell: at the time it was really dominated by one person, and if you didn't work with that person, you couldn't be part of the program. So I, like a lot of other folks who didn't quite fit, found other communities, queer and feminist communities, and held our own readings and workshops.

As far as formal practices, I never thought I would write a book of haiku. And I am quite aware that what I have written does not necessarily even fit the category as currently defined by many writers and critics of haiku, in this country at least: they have titles, they follow strict syllabic rules, they are less about simple moments of discovery or wonder and more about complex moments of embodiment, medicalization, survival, and loss. I very much did not plan to write haiku. But once I started, the syllabic structure became so crucial to me. It seemed almost impossible to say what I needed to say in so few syllables. Everything had to be compressed so tightly. But by forcing myself to stay inside that form, I gained back some of the sense of control that was slipping away from me at the time. And the poems took me to places I never expected to go either, like talking about my mother, or Narcissus, or the garden of Eden. I think form in poetry is incredibly generative when it allows you go to a place you didn't know you were trying to find, rather than laying out a predetermined path you think you have to follow. That's what this haiku form ended up doing for me.

Speaking of monikers, what does your title represent? How was it generated? Talk about the way you titled the book, and how your process of naming (individual pieces, sections, etc.) influences you and/ or colors your work specifically.

The titles of the individual poems are really important because the poems themselves are so short and compressed, so the title is also doing a lot of the meaning-making of each poem. I chose for the most part titles from medical terminology, which tends to the impersonal, to act as a kind of foil to the very intense personal experiences explored in the poems themselves. The same is somewhat true of the section titles: "Symptoms and Signs" is taken straight from the language used for medical records or diagnostic criteria. "Coloring the Pain Book" describes the literal experience of what often happens in pain clinics where you, the patient, are given markers and an outline of a body and told to color all the places you hurt with colors that match the type of pain: numb, burning, stabbing, etc. I have colored dozens of those over the years. But also of course that title is doing some metaphorical work also: This book is a "Pain Book" as well, and we are coloring it together, me by writing the poems and you by reading them.

I wasn't sure what to call the book for a long time: *Hypermobilities* seemed too obvious. But over time I realized it was the right title. Ehlers-Danlos Syndrome is a genetic condition that causes faulty collagen, so it affects pretty much all the body's systems. But joint hypermobility is the hallmark sign of the condition and the most common type of EDS is Hypermobility type. I actually am not diagnosed with Hypermobility type, but with the less common Classical type. But the truth is, they really don't know what type I have: As I talk about in the essay, I have features of Hypermobility, Classical, and Vascular types, but my genetic testing has ruled out Vascular and been inconclusive on Classical. I spend a lot of time explaining this to new doctors. I do have extremely hypermobile joints however, and like many of us with EDS, I used to think these were just oddities of my particular body until I was finally diagnosed at age thirty-five. Now I live with the fact that at any moment one of my joints could just slip out of place, causing injuries that usually would only happen in car accidents or intense contact sports. It happens if I turn my head the wrong way. It happens in my sleep. I hate it but also I have to find a way to love it because it is the body I have, the body I am. I can't live hating myself all the time. And so in a way this book, *Hypermobilities*, is about moving between those worlds, slipping between them like a joint from its socket, looking at myself reflected in the words and trying to love what I see there even when it hurts the most.

What does this particular work represent to you as indicative of your method/creative practice? your history? of your mission/intentions/hopes/plans?

I think of poetry as like singing, and my poems sing themselves into existence through me. I don't consciously design them, I don't plan them out like I do a work of critical analysis. I never expected to write this book. I am working on three or four books now, and two of them I can plan out and make outlines for: one is a research monograph and one is a hybrid critical/creative nonfiction book. But the third one, a collection of personal essays, I have no idea when it will be done or what essays will end up in it because I am only learning about them as I write them, and some I have been writing for years and they're still not done, they might never get done.

It's very hard in some ways to give up that control, and it also is difficult in academia where I'm always being asked to account for my work, to give publishing timelines and stick to them. But I am often just too sick to do the kind of research-intense writing that the monographs require and so I end up doing more creative writing because that's more what my bodymind is able to manage. So I am also writing more poems these days than I expected and perhaps I will have another poetry collection in a year or two. I am trying very hard to just accept what comes and remember what is essential about my writing and what is not (external deadlines, publish-or-perish, etc.).

What does this book DO (as much as what it says or contains)?

I think on the most basic level, this book says to the reader "welcome to my world." As in, *see what it is like to live with my bodymind, my experience,* but also as in, *welcome, I want to know you, I want you to know me.* It is about writing out of isolation in order to make connections at the very sites that are designed to separate us from each other: the boundaries of our bodies, the loneliness of the exam room, the impersonalization of medical languages.

What would be the best possible outcome for this book? What might it do in the world, and how will its presence as an object facilitate your creative role in your community and beyond? What are your hopes for this book, and for your practice?

I have this dream that some people with Ehlers-Danlos Syndrome will read this book and find that it speaks to their experience, that it makes them feel less alone. Although many more people are being diagnosed with EDS since the diagnostic criteria were revised in 2017, it's still a very lonely disease to have. Most doctors aren't trained about it. Most people haven't heard of it. So if my poems help temper that isolation for some people, that would make me so glad. Also of course I hope these poems speak to many other people without EDS-both those with other chronic illnesses or disabilities, and those without. I hope to give readings, both in person and virtual, in poetry contexts but also in disability and medical contexts, always just seeking to get my words out to as many people as possible in hopes that for some people, they will make a difference.

What does it mean to make books in this time, and what are your thoughts around shifting into digital books/objects and digital access in general?

I love print books and it was very important to me for *Hypermobilities* to be published as a physical book. I love buying people's books, reading them, having them on my shelf where I can find them again. I have a lot of trouble reading long works on screens, both physically and cognitively. But it is also so important to have books available digitally, for access to people with disabilities that make reading physical print difficult or impossible, and for economic and geographic access. I don't want us to shift to an all-digital publishing world, but I think a hybrid approach is absolutely crucial for all kinds of access moving forward.

Let's talk a little bit about the role of poetics and creative community in social and political activism, so present in our daily lives as we face the often sobering, sometimes dangerous realities of the Capitalocene. The publication of this volume now falls during an ongoing global pandemic, intersecting with the largest collective uprising in US history, with Black Lives Matter, dismantling white supremacy, and abolition at the fore. How does your process, practice, or work reflect these conditions?

Well, I talked about this a bit earlier, in terms of using my privilege to uplift and support multiply marginalized sick and disabled writers, especially disabled and neurodivergent BIPOC writers. Do I think my book engages directly with some of these crucial struggles? Certainly not as much as my scholarship, which is very directly engaged in anti-racist, radical crip worldmaking. It is a book written from deep inside my own body, and its very conditions of creation meant I was at home or in the hospital instead of out in the streets where I would have been when I was younger and healthier. But I have found that writing the raw truth of my disabled experience, as honestly and also humbly as I can, can sometimes be useful to others with whom I claim solidarity and so I hope this book can be useful as well.

I'd be curious to hear some of your thoughts on the challenges we face in speaking and publishing across lines of race, age, ability, class, privilege, social/cultural background, gender, sexuality (and other identifiers) within the community as well as creating and maintaining safe spaces, vs. the dangers of remaining and producing in isolated "silos" and/or disciplinary and/or institutional bounds?

I think it's all about the difference between speaking "with," rather than "for" or "as." We have to be able to speak and write with each other, across our differences, as Audre Lorde wrote about so powerfully back in the 1970s and 1980s. But we must be very careful about who we claim to speak "for," and I think it is even more complicated to try to speak "as" someone else whose positionality we do not share. I don't write fiction-everything I write is like me, me, my friends, my dog, what I had for dinner-so I don't have good insight into how to ethically write fictional characters across difference, though certainly as a literary scholar I could point to some people who I think do so very brilliantly, like Toni Morrison for example, and many who do so quite problematically, who I won't bother to name.

I do in my scholarship write about people who are quite different from me-I am writing right now about two pairs of sisters, Millie and Christine McKoy and Yvonne and Yvette McCarther, who were African American conjoined twins from the 19th and mid-20th centuries-and I try very hard to be clear I am not claiming I can speak for them or that our experiences are at all the same. But I do believe that I can and even must speak and act in solidarity with them, as a disabled person, as a person with a condition shared by many "freak show" performers of the past, and as a white person in this country who, like all of us, bears a responsibility for reckoning with history and for imagining and working toward new futures.

The Operating System uses the language "print/document" to differentiate from the book-object as part of our mission to distinguish the act of documentation-in-book-FORM from the act of publishing as a backwards-facing replication of the book's agentive *role* as it may have appeared the last several centuries of its history. Ultimately, I approach the book as TECHNOLOGY: one of a variety of printed documents (in this case, bound) that humans have invented and in turn used to archive and disseminate ideas, beliefs, stories, and other evidence of production.

Ownership and use of printing presses and access to (or restriction of printed materials) has long been a site of struggle, related in many ways to revolutionary activity and the fight for civil rights and free speech all over the world. While (in many countries) the contemporary quotidian landscape has indeed drastically shifted in its access to platforms for sharing information and in the widespread ability to "publish" digitally, even with extremely limited resources, the importance of publication on physical media has not diminished. In fact, this may be the most critical time in recent history for activist groups, artists, and others to insist upon learning, establishing, and encouraging personal and community documentation practices. Hear me out.

With The OS's print endeavors I wanted to open up a conversation about this: the ultimately radical, transgressive act of creating PRINT / DOCUMENTATION in the digital age. It's a question of the archive, and of history: who gets to tell the story, and what evidence of our life, our behaviors, our experiences are we leaving behind? We can know little to nothing about the future into which we're leaving an unprecedentedly digital document trail — but we can be assured that publications, government agencies, museums, schools, and other institutional powers that be will continue to leave BOTH a digital and print version of their production for the official record. Will we?

As a (rogue) anthropologist and long time academic, I can easily pull up many accounts about how lives, behaviors, experiences — how THE STORY of a time or place — was pieced together using the deep study of correspondence, notebooks, and other physical documents which are no longer the norm in many lives and practices. As we move our creative behaviors towards digital note taking, and even audio and video, what can we predict about future technology that is in any way assuring that our stories will be accurately told – or told at all? How will we leave these things for the record? In these documents we say:

WE WERE HERE, WE EXISTED, WE HAVE A DIFFERENT STORY

- *Elæ Moss, Founder/Creative Director*

2020-21

UNLIMITED EDITIONS

Institution is a Verb: A Panoply Performance Lab Compilation - Esther Neff, Ayana Evans, Tsedaye Makonnen and Elizabeth Lamb, editors.
Daughter Isotope - Vidhu Aggarwal
Failure Biographies - Johnny Damm
Ginger Ko - Power ON
Danielle Pafunda - Spite
Robert Balun - Acid Western

KIN(D)* TEXTS AND PROJECTS

Intergalactic Travels: Poems from a Fugutive Alien - Alan Pelaez Lopez
HOAX - Joey De Jesus [Kin(d)*]
RoseSunWater - Angel Dominguez [Kin(d)*/Glossarium]
Bodies of Work - Elæ Moss & Georgia Elrod

GLOSSARIUM: UNSILENCED TEXTS AND TRANSLATIONS

Manhatitlán [Glossarium] - Steven Alvarez
Híkurí (Peyote) - José Vincente Anaya (tr. Joshua Pollock)
Vormorgen - Ersnt Toller tr. Mathilda Cullen [Glossarium x Kin(d)*; German-English]
Black and Blue Partition ('Mistry) - Monchoachi tr. Patricia Hartland [Glossarium; French & Antillean Creole/English]

IN CORPORE SANO

Hypermobilities - Ellen Samuels
Goodbye Wolf-Nik DeDominic

2019

UNLIMITED EDITIONS

Ark Hive-Marthe Reed
I Made for You a New Machine and All it Does is Hope -
Richard Lucyshyn
Illusory Borders-Heidi Reszies
A Year of Misreading the Wildcats - Orchid Tierney
Of Color: Poets' Ways of Making | An Anthology of Essays on
Transformative Poetics - Amanda Galvan Huynh &
Luisa A. Igloria, Editors

KIN(D)* TEXTS AND PROJECTS

A Bony Framework for the Tangible Universe-D. Allen [In Corpore
Sano]
Opera on TV-James Brunton
Hall of Waters-Berry Grass
Transitional Object-Adrian Silbernagel

GLOSSARIUM: UNSILENCED TEXTS AND TRANSLATIONS

Śnienie / Dreaming - Marta Zelwan/Krystyna Sakowicz,
(Poland, trans. Victoria Miluch)
High Tide Of The Eyes - Bijan Elahi (Farsi-English/dual-language)
trans. Rebecca Ruth Gould and Kayvan Tahmasebian
In the Drying Shed of Souls: Poetry from Cuba's Generation Zero
Katherine Hedeen and Víctor Rodríguez Núñez, translators/editors
Street Gloss - Brent Armendinger with translations of Alejandro
Méndez, Mercedes Roffé, Fabián Casas, Diana Bellessi
& Néstor Perlongher (Argentina)
Operation on a Malignant Body - Sergio Loo
(Mexico, trans. Will Stockton)[In Corpore Sano]
Are There Copper Pipes in Heaven - Katrin Ottarsdóttir
(Faroe Islands, trans. Matthew Landrum)

DOCUMENT

/däkyəmənt/
First meant "instruction" or "evidence," whether written or not.

noun - a piece of written, printed, or electronic matter that provides information or evidence or that serves as an official record
verb - record (something) in written, photographic, or other form
synonyms - paper - deed - record - writing - act - instrument

[*Middle English, precept, from Old French, from Latin documentum, example, proof, from docre, to teach; see dek- in Indo-European roots.*]

Who is responsible for the manufacture of value?

Based on what supercilious ontology have we landed in a space where we vie against other creative people in vain pursuit of the fleeting credibilities of the scarcity economy, rather than freely collaborating and sharing openly with each other in ecstatic celebration of MAKING?

While we understand and acknowledge the economic pressures and fear-mongering that threatens to dominate and crush the creative impulse, we also believe that *now more than ever* *we have the tools to redistribute agency via cooperative means,* fueled by the fires of the Open Source Movement.

Looking out across the invisible vistas of that rhizomatic parallel country we can begin to see our community beyond constraints, in the place where intention meets resilient, proactive, collaborative organization.

Here is a document born of that belief, sown purely of imagination and will. When we document we assert. We print to make real, to reify our being there. When we do so with mindful intention to address our process, to open our work to others, to create beauty in words in space, to respect and acknowledge the strength of the page we now hold physical, a thing in our hand, we remind ourselves that, like Dorothy: *we had the power all along, my dears.*

the PRINT! DOCUMENT SERIES

is a project of
the trouble with bartleby
in collaboration with
the operating system